THE SECOND BLESSING

A GUIDEBOOK FOR
RECEIVING THE BAPTISM
IN THE HOLY SPIRIT

KURT D. STRATTON

HISPUBLISHING GROUP

www.hispubg.com
A division of HISpecialists, llc

HIS Publishing Group
4310 Wiley Post Rd., Suite 201D
Addison, Texas 75001
info@hispubg.com

ISBN-13: 978-0-578-18912-3

The Second Blessing/Kurt D. Stratton — 1st ed.
10 9 8 7 6 5 4 3 2

Cover art by Kurt Stratton

Printed in the United States of America

TABLE OF CONTENTS

ACKNOWLEDGMENTS

M Y DEEPEST THANKS TO THE LATE Captain, Chaplain Dr. Stanford E. Linzey, Jr., U.S.N., my former chaplain on the U.S.S. Coral Sea in Vietnam, who laid hands on me to receive this wonderful gift, and later supported my ministry as a young pastor.

Thank you to my patient and loving wife, Carolyn, who believes more in me than I do myself. She inspires me daily to love the Lord with all my heart and use all my gifts for His glory.

And thank you to Linda Perry whose career as an English educator was very helpful in editing this guidebook.

INTRODUCTION

T HE SECOND BLESSING CHANGED MY life. Granted, the First Blessing transformed me in God's eyes—from a sinner to a saint; a child of wrath to a son of God; a lost soul to one whose name is written in the Lamb's Book of Life. That first blessing changed my eternal position. The second blessing changed my earthly power.

Now, that blessing affects the way I worship, pray, give, witness and even look at life. In these pages I will uncover the promises of God to empower your life and discover the Lord Jesus Christ as The Baptizer in the Holy Spirit.

Chapter One

MY STORY

WHAT DID OUR FAMILY OF FOUR brothers and three sisters have in common? Just Mom and Dad. We were as different as night and day. So when it was my time to go out into the world I knew college was not for me. But I needed to avoid the draft in 1971 so I joined the Navy. I figured that would be safe. Not a chance.

Just before graduating high school, my friend Victor told me the Gospel of Jesus Christ. It sounded so good. No one had ever explained God's grace to me before, and that I could not earn or deserve eternal life on my own good works. (Our religion never mentioned being saved. It just said that if you kept certain rituals and lived a good life, you'd find out if you made it to heaven when you died. But I thought, if God loves us, wouldn't He give us some assurance now?).

So, what did I do after I heard about grace? I ran the other way. As soon as the seed settled on my heart, the devil plucked it up saying, "You'll have to give up everything, put on a white robe, go sit on a hill and chant" (which many young people were doing in communes and cults at that time). Well, I certainly didn't want that. But God was going to get my attention one way or another. Within weeks, I was involved in a head-on collision in which my head put a large hole in the windshield. My friend Dave was just driving me down the street to the auto parts store so I didn't bother putting on his greasy seat belt. When he ran the yellow/red light, a 16-year-old-newly-licensed driver turned right in front of us at the intersection of 9 Mile Road and Grand River in Farmington, Michigan. In a split second, I put my hands on the dashboard and saw my life pass before me. My head hit the windshield, and I was thrown back into the seat as my arms acted as giant shock absorbers. I didn't feel a thing. But I looked up at the gaping hole in the passenger's side of the windshield on Dave's 1966 Mustang fastback, looked over at woozy Dave, and said, "Did you do that?" As I shook my head shards of glass went everywhere. Strangely, I wasn't hurt, but I remember saying "Oh, God, I'm sorry." But since I didn't know about repentance, I did not change. This was the same intersection where I used to work flipping pizzas at Romano's Restaurant. Ronnie Hand, the owner, drove up right after I tumbled out of the smashed up car and was sitting on the curb with my head in my hands. He helped me up, put me on the restaurant floor and called an ambulance. I could feel my body going into shock so I talked myself out of it. I said, "You were in an accident, but you'll be alright. Just breathe slowly and deeply and everything will be fine." An ambulance came and put me in the passenger's seat! They ushered me into a cubicle at the ER, drew the curtain around it and forgot about me. After an hour I shouted "Hey! Anybody there?" The nurse came running over and said, "Oh! We forgot about you." After digging a piece of glass out of my head, and dabbing the small wound, they sent me home.

Two weeks later, my other buddy, Andy, and I were stopped at an intersection in Southfield, MI. There was an 18-wheeler on my right, so when the light turned green, I didn't see the elderly man running his red light. Andy, an all-state wrestler, saw the car speeding towards us, and jumped into the back seat. Something told me to turn towards the other car and step on the gas. It prevented us from being broadsided and doing some serious damage. Instead, my car was side-swiped and we spun around in the intersection. Andy was in midair when we were struck, and bounced around like a Superball. When we finally stopped, I shook tiny pieces of glass off all my clothing. Again, I wasn't hurt. Again, I said "Oh, God, I'm sorry." Andy's ribs were bruised, so we waited for an ambulance for him. A state trooper arrived and accused me of causing the accident. But when I went over to the truck driver to ask for help, he didn't say a word, just handed me a clipboard with a diagram of the intersection with Car A and Car B, arrows, and my green light, and the other guy's red light. I looked up at him in awe and stuttered, "Th-thank you, Mister." The trooper didn't like being wrong, and snarled, "You're lucky you have a witness."

While waiting for Andy to get patched up at the hospital, my dad got word of the accident. His phone call found me in the cafeteria, and he asked me three times "Are you okay?" After I assured him I was fine, he then lowered his voice in that parental tone and asked, "How's the car?" "Well," I said, "that's not so good." It was totaled just like the car two weeks earlier.

In 1970, soon after high school, I won the Lottery. No, not that one. This was the government lottery by birthday to see who would be drafted into the U.S. Army. My number was 92, and they were taking up to 130. So, I thought, "Well, Momma didn't raise any dummies. I'll join the Navy so I won't go to 'Nam."

Next stop—Vietnam. Our homeport was the Philippine Islands. I had never been away from home. So, when I was off duty, I was free to do whatever I wanted, and I did. At nineteen years of age, I was burning myself out with partying and bad company. But when we were on the ship, there were strong believers showing me the power and joy of the Christian life. Often, we would stand in a puddle of sweat loading bomb fins and supplies. Bill Aswegan and Bob Brainerd would be on either side of me saying, "Well, praise the

Lord. This is great exercise. Isn't God good!" If they weren't both bigger than me, I would have put their lights out. But, I desperately wanted what they had. Only, I didn't want to give up anything at the same time.

Then on April 5, 1972, as a radioman onboard the U.S.S. Coral Sea, I received a casualty report as I had so many other times. But this one was from our sister ship right next to us. She took a direct hit on her gunmount. Fifty two sailors were injured, and nine were instantly killed.

After my watch, I was looking out over the ocean that night. It seemed so peaceful. No one was shooting or firing missiles or even flying jets. While I was minding my own business, a question popped into my mind out of nowhere: "How long can you keep living like you're living?" I reasoned, "Probably not past thirty," realizing I was burning out my body, and frequenting some dangerous places. And then another question: "Where would you be right now if you were one of those nine men killed today?" It suddenly dawned on me that God was speaking directly to my heart. I answered: "I wouldn't be with You, would I?"

At that point, I couldn't hold it in any longer. I got angry with God. I said, "You've been after me for the past year and a half. You've chased me clear across the other side of the world. Every time I turn around, you have Your people in my face. I'm tired of running from You. If You are real, and Jesus is alive, here I am. I give up!"

Well, I was raised to believe that if you talked like that to God, you were going to get it! So, even at my wit's end, I was prepared for the worst. But suddenly, literally, I felt arms wrap around me, and a peaceful voice speaking to my heart: "Kurt, I accept you just as you are." And then in just a fraction of a second, the Lord allowed me to see and understand His unconditional love for me.

That night as I lay in my rack, I asked the Lord to help me change my lifestyle. I gave up my sailor's ways. I wasn't sure what to expect, but the next morning I woke up and was completely set free from my addictions to drinking, smoking and cussing. I was a "new creature. Old things had passed away. Behold, all things had become new" (2 Cor. 5:17). Unlike so many others, I couldn't tell you that I was saved in a particular church, or at a revival meeting. All I could do would be to give you longitude and latitude for the middle of the Tonkin Gulf.

I found a Bible and began devouring the words of eternal life. That's all I read, day and night. I found other brothers and told them I had accepted Jesus. At first, they were suspicious, knowing how wild I had been. But they saw the outward change immediately and soon embraced me into the group. But my old drinking buddies said, 'Yeah, we've seen this before. You got religion, but it won't last.'

When we came back to the States, I was told of a Bible-believing church close to the San Francisco airport. The pastor was an excellent preacher, but every once in a while he would say something against the Holy Spirit and those who practice spiritual gifts. It was strange, but I still remember cringing inside. I didn't know that was the grieving of the Spirit.

Just before my second Vietnam tour, the pastor pulled me aside to warn me: 'Kurt, stay away from those Pentecostal people.' But he didn't explain why, so my curiosity was piqued.

Back on the ship in Nam, I was standing in one of our long chow lines, next to Frank Klapach (who later became a Navy Chaplain for the Assemblies of God). We were just talking about the goodness of God when he asked if I had been "baptized in the Holy Spirit." I said I received the Holy Spirit when I got saved. He explained that the baptism was different and came after salvation, and was accompanied by the demonstration of spiritual gifts. I said derisively, "You mean like speaking in tongues? Yeah, well, I don't believe in that." Frank didn't bat an eye, but patiently asked, "And why is that?" Well, I didn't have the guts to say that my pastor told me to stay away from the likes of him, so I just repeated that I didn't believe in that.

Frank was not deterred. He said, 'Every Thursday at 7:30 p.m., we have a Pentecostal/Charismatic prayer meeting in the Library Chapel. I'd like to invite you to come when you can. You might find it very interesting.'

"Yeah, sure," I thought. "There was no way I was going to be sucked into that demon-influenced group." But the more I protested in my mind, the more the Lord began to draw me to that meeting. So, for the first time in my life as a believer, I put a "fleece" before the Lord. I said, "Dear Lord, if this is of You, when I walk down to the Library Chapel, if no one says Hi to me or even speaks with me on the way,

I'll know the baptism in the Holy Spirit is from You, and is for me." I knew about a thousand men on our ship, and I was going to walk through the chow hall at dinner time. Someone would surely talk to me.

As I walked through the chow hall, I saw guys I knew, who looked right at me but turned away. Right through the whole chow hall and not a single Hi!

Now, I stood at the door of the Library Chapel and was about to turn tail and run. But the Lord spoke to my heart, "I met your fleece, now go in." And I obeyed, but was petrified at the same time.

What I heard that evening was life-changing. Sailors and officers were worshipping the Lord in "psalms, hymns and spiritual songs, making melody in their hearts unto the Lord." And the strangest thing of all, I heard these sailors singing in harmony in languages I had never heard before. It was beautiful. (Ladies, if you want to hear something you'll never forget, just listen to a group of men singing in the Spirit).

When the service was over, Chaplain Stan Linzey asked if he could pray that I might receive the baptism in the Holy Spirit. I clammed up and said, "No, I'm not ready yet." I didn't have the heart to tell him about the Lord meeting my fleece. Chaplain Linzey was a large man who had survived the sinking of the USS Yorktown by the Japanese in June, 1944, and he leaned over, pointed a big finger in my face and boldly said, "It's not that you're not ready, you just don't want to step out in faith." Well, where I'm from, that was as good as a triple-dog dare. So, he had the nerve to ask me again, "Do you want us to pray that you might be baptized in the Holy Spirit?" I took a big gulp and said, "Yes."

Chaplain Linzey and Frank Klapach laid hands on me as they were praising the Lord and simply said, "Be filled with the Spirit." The next thing I knew, I was speaking words I had never heard before. Linzey said, "That's it! Keep it up! You've got it!" And with that confirmation, the words began to flow. After a few minutes of praising the Lord in my new language, I stopped. The chaplain looked at me with a big grin and said, "Well, what do you think?" All I could say was "Zoom!"

I remember going up to my rack, getting into bed and speaking in my new language quietly. I couldn't sleep. The Lord was so close to me. I sensed a joy and power I had never known. God touched me…me!

One week later, I was sitting in that same chair in the Library/Chapel, praying, when the Lord spoke to my heart again, "I want you to preach the Gospel full-time." That was it. No fanfare. No earthquake. But I knew it was the Lord.

Did you know that God has a great sense of humor? I had always believed that professional clergy were guys who couldn't get a regular job in the real world, so they went and hid in the church. And now, the Lord was calling me to preach the Gospel full-time.

From that moment on, I set my face to pursue His calling, because our Father will always give us a heart to obey His will. I found a Bible college in Santa Cruz, California, graduated as the Class Speaker in 1978, later went to seminary, and entered the ministry. Since then, I have been a youth pastor, senior pastor of four churches, home missionary, religion columnist, Christian broadcaster, author of KURT'S DAILY MUSE (an Internet devotional), and founding minister of Spirit Life Clinic.

One of the greatest gifts the Lord has given me is my wonderful wife, Carolyn. She was reared as a preacher's kid in the Baptist faith. As an adult, she married a Baptist pastor, who was the senior minister at a Dallas church for 21 years until a traffic accident claimed his life. Shortly after that, my friend Clint Pruett called me late one night to say that he had just met my future wife. I asked why he wasn't interested in her. "She's out of my league," he confessed. Apparently, he had taken her out for coffee and halfway through their date, he kept seeing a picture of Carolyn and me together. He just couldn't shake it. So, at 11:30 p.m., Clint awakened me to share the good news of meeting this woman. Two days later I talked with Carolyn for two hours on the phone, sang to her my happy song ("Heaven Came Down"), and knew that God would put us together. Within five months, we were married. Clint was my best man, and a year later I performed his wedding!

So here we were a Baptist/Pentecostal couple. But Carolyn loved me and loved the Lord Jesus Christ even more. Soon afterwards, during the invitation at one of my Spirit Life Clinics, to my great joy, Carolyn came down to the altar. I laid hands on her and she was baptized in the

Holy Spirit, speaking out the language of the spirit that had been inside her for most of her life!

Through it all, I can say without hesitation, God is faithful to His Word, for "ye shall receive power after the Holy Ghost has come upon you."

Chapter Two

THE BAPTISM IN THE HOLY SPIRIT

🪽

THE BAPTISM IN THE HOLY SPIRIT IS for you. It is for everybody. It is for "all flesh!" That means, if you are in a body, it is for you. God does not show favoritism. This is a common teaching for common people, because in Jesus' culture, He was a common man. Contrary to many church methods, it is not difficult, but understandable and simple. The purpose of this book is to show that the gift of the Spirit is for you, and you can receive it at any time. Our human nature wants to work for everything, but this is a gift for those of a child-like faith.

WHAT CAN YOU EXPECT WHEN YOU PRAY TO RECEIVE THE BAPTISM?

» To be filled with the Holy Spirit and speak in tongues (the initial evidence)
» A "time of refreshing" which you may have never experienced before
» Power to be a witness for Jesus, and the joy to go with it
» An open door for all the spiritual gifts (prophecy, faith, healings, miracles, word of knowledge, word of wisdom, discernment of spirits, and interpretation of tongues)
» Personal healing and deliverance.

THIS BOOK HAS A TWO-FOLD PURPOSE

» To guide believers in being filled with the Holy Spirit.
» And to give a biblical background concerning the Baptism in the Holy Spirit.

Please remember, only Jesus Christ is the Baptizer.

IN THIS BOOK, I'LL ANSWER THESE QUESTIONS AND DISPEL MANY MISCONCEPTIONS

» Does a person need to be emotional to receive the Baptism in the Holy Spirit?

» When one speaks in tongues, does the Holy Spirit speak through him?

» Must it be an articulate language?

» Is babbling ever done, and how can you tell?

» Can one receive a false experience or counterfeit gift?

» Does the Devil speak in tongues?

» Is holiness necessary for receiving the Baptism in the Holy Spirit?

» How old should one be to receive the Baptism?

» Why speak with tongues?

» What comes after the Baptism?

God will not play favorites. That is a pivotal truth. Everyone who comes to Jesus by faith, expecting, will be saved and filled with His Spirit.

"And it shall come to pass afterward that I will pour out My Spirit on all

flesh; your sons and your daughters shall prophesy, your old men shall dream dreams, your young men shall see visions. And also on My menservants and on My maidservants I will pour out My Spirit in those days….And it shall come to pass that whoever calls on the name of the Lord shall be saved." (Joel 2:28, 29, 32)

In the above passage, it includes "all flesh;" family members, both men and women, the elderly, the young, and the poor.

"No good thing will He withhold from those who walk uprightly." (Psalms 84:11)

In Matthew 3:1-11 John the Baptist came preaching repentance and baptizing in water. Then he said, "He who is coming after me…He will baptize you with the Holy Spirit and fire."

THERE ARE THREE MAJOR BAPTISMS

MENTIONED IN THE BIBLE

1. Water Baptism. This is a command for each believer to publicly confess Jesus Christ as one's personal Lord and Savior, and to identify with Christ's death, burial and resurrection to a new life in Him.

"Therefore we were buried with Him through baptism into death, that just as Christ was raised from the dead by the glory of the Father, even so we also should walk in newness of life." (Romans 6:4)

2. Baptism into the Body of Christ by the Holy Spirit. This is where we become members of His Church.

"For by one Spirit we were all baptized into one body—whether Jews or Greeks, whether slaves or free—and have been made to drink into one Spirit." (I Corinthians 12:13)

Also, this is when the Holy Spirit comes to dwell inside each believer.

3. Baptism by Christ into the Holy Spirit

(found in each Gospel account and Acts 11:16). This is a second blessing whereby believers are filled to overflowing with the Holy Spirit, evidenced by speaking in tongues, which can happen at the moment of salvation or afterwards.

All Christians have the Holy Spirit. "....Now if anyone does not have the Spirit of Christ, he is not His" (Romans 8:9). But the Holy Spirit does not have all Christians. That one statement can be a turning point in receiving the Baptism in the Spirit.

> *"I send the Promise of My Father upon you; but tarry in Jerusalem until you are endued with power from on high."*
> *(Luke 24:49)*

In old-time Pentecost, seekers would tarry for days, months, even years for the Baptism. This is not necessary. In fact, it can harm your faith, and make you feel less than worthy. In this text, the believers were told to wait until the Feast of Pentecost came (fifty days after the Passover). That was necessary to have the most Jews in Jerusalem to witness the outpouring of the Spirit and the beginning of the Church. But nowhere in Scripture are we told to tarry for the Baptism.

> "On the last day, that great day of the feast, Jesus stood and cried out, saying, "If anyone thirsts, let him come to Me and drink. He who believes in Me, as the Scripture has said, out of his heart will flow rivers of living water." But this He spoke concerning the Spirit, whom those believing in Him would receive; for the Holy Spirit was not yet given, because Jesus was not yet glorified." (John 7:37-39)

Where does the Holy Spirit come from? Yes, inside you (not light years away from some other galaxy). When Christians realize that, they get filled with the Spirit in a moment's time.

Let me use an illustration here. Picture a glass of water filled halfway. That represents you being saved. It is subjective—"You are saved. Your sins are forgiven. Your name is written in heaven, etc." But take that same glass and fill it to overflowing. Now it affects the outside of the glass, the floor, and runs out into the street. It is objective—affecting the world around you.

This is the difference between being saved and being baptized with the Spirit. One is for you, the other is to equip and empower you to serve the Lord and others. (This will always be an obstacle to lukewarm believers).

Linguists tell us that our language is stored up in our minds. But our spirit language is stored up in our spirit. Once we discover our new language, it will flow just as easily as our native tongue.

When we get right with God, the lines of communication are open, aren't they? Yes, the Holy Spirit is said to be our Comforter, Teacher, Guide, Corrector, and Equipper for all good works.

When you pray and communicate with God, you sometimes "groan" in the spirit, right? That comes from your spirit, in fellowship with God. You are bypassing your mind.

> "…but whoever drinks of the water that I shall give him will never thirst. But the water that I shall give him will become in him a fountain of water springing up into everlasting life." (John 4:14)

If you've prayed and haven't received the Baptism, you wonder 'What's wrong with me?' And especially if someone who isn't as "good" as you gets the whole ball of wax at once!

Please understand, there are no second-class citizens in the Kingdom of God. And those who have the Baptism are not better than those who don't have it. All you can say is that when you receive "you are better than you were before." But not everyone may like the new and improved you.

In 1984, I was a student at Golden Gate Baptist Theological Seminary in Mill Valley, California. In our Worship 101 class the professor asked, "How many here are Baptists?" About 90 students out of 100 raised their hands. "How many mainline denominations are here?" About nine raised their hands. Finally, he asked, "How many Pentecostals?" I was the only hand.

After class, I was cornered by a fellow student named Brian in the hallway, asking if we could meet later to talk about the Baptism. (I figured the Baptist seminary might frown on me laying hands on students and praying in tongues in the hallways).

Brian came to my apartment. I went through the teaching on the Baptism in the Holy Spirit in about 20 minutes, laid hands on him, and he wonderfully received, fluently speaking in tongues. The Holy Spirit changed his life. And every time I saw him at school after that, he was on fire. But, he confessed that his dyed-in-the-wool fundamentalist wife was having a difficult time with his new-found liberty in the Spirit and speaking in tongues. (A word of caution: When many first receive the Baptism, they tend to get zealous about this new experience, and overstep the wisdom and timing of the Lord).

What can you expect when you are initially filled with the Holy Spirit?

Aside from the obvious speaking with new tongues, you may also receive a refreshing in your spirit and a new boldness in your faith. Also, don't be surprised if you start confessing sins, prejudices and jealousies.

When I was still in the Navy, while in the Philippines, Columban college in Olongapo City invited us Pentecostal sailors to come and teach on the Baptism in the Holy Spirit. One young lady, Lydia, came up to me after the lesson and asked, "Kurt, do you give the Holy Spirit?" I smiled at her innocence and said, "If you mean, do I minister the Baptism, yes." "I want that!" So, one of our Pentecostal brothers, Jim Hough (who later became a military chaplain and one of the translators of the Modern English Version of the Bible - MEV) and I set up a time to meet with her two days later. We then went through the teaching, laid hands on her, and she beautifully received. Then, she felt a strong need to confess that when Filipinos saw Americans, they saw two colors: White, which is superior, and green which is money, which supported her hometown. Later, she wrote me a letter saying that before she received the Baptism, she thought it was her duty to become a nun, but felt now the Lord was leading her in a different direction.

I have a method for ministering the Baptism. It may not be the best, but it has worked for me. If your method hasn't worked you might want to try mine. But I'm straight-forward, no-nonsense, and I believe God for results. I do not give the Holy Spirit; only Jesus Christ can baptize with His Spirit. But God does use me as I lay hands on people, and by faith they receive, with the evidence of speaking in tongues. (Some reading this will receive as they step out in faith and start praising the Lord right now, allowing Him to fill them to overflowing).

> *"When the Day of Pentecost had fully come, they were all with one accord in one place. And suddenly there came a sound from heaven, as of a rushing mighty wind, and it filled the whole house where they were sitting. Then there appeared to them divided tongues, as of fire, and one sat upon each of them. And they were all filled with the Holy Spirit and began to speak with other tongues, as the Spirit gave them utterance." (Acts 2:1-4)*

> *"But you shall receive power when the Holy Spirit has come upon you, and you shall be witnesses to Me...to the end of the earth." (Acts 1:8)*

> *"And these signs will follow those who believe; In My name they will cast out*

demons, they will speak with new tongues; they will take up serpents; and if they drink anything deadly, it will by no means hurt them; they will lay hands on the sick, and they will recover." (Mark 16:17)

Some will argue: "You Pentecostals are always seeking tongues." Yes, that's exactly right. I make no apologies for seeking everything the Lord has for me—not just tongues, but healings, miracles, discernment of spirits, words of knowledge and wisdom, etc.—all the gifts so that Jesus Christ might be glorified!

LET ME DISPEL SOME ARGUMENTS

1. Some would say: "In Acts 2, they preached the Gospel in tongues because people were ignorant and couldn't read." Read it again. It says they were "speaking the wonderful works of God." But Peter stood up and did preach the Gospel in his own language.

2. Others say: "Tongues and spiritual gifts have passed away with the apos-

tles." Really? Show me the scriptures that support that claim. Peter, in Acts 2:17, quoted Joel 2:28-32 *"It shall come to pass in the last days, says God, 'That I will pour out of My Spirit on ALL flesh..."* That means you and me.

3. Then some say: "You have to be saved first before you can receive the Baptism." Read about Cornelius in Acts 10. His whole household was saved and baptized in the Holy Spirit at the same time.

My friend was preaching at a small church near Long Beach, California. A sailor was there because his girlfriend went to the church, and her parents would not permit them to date unless he attended their church. The sailor was not a believer. So, when the invitation to receive the Baptism in the Holy Spirit was given, the sailor came forward. As he was coming down the aisle, one dear old saint in the back whispered loudly, "He's not even saved." The preacher just ignored her, laid hands on the young man, and this sailor bowed his head and squeezed his eyes shut very tightly, as if in pain, then suddenly lifted his head, threw his hands up and shouted, "God, save me, save me!" and started talking in tongues right in front of the whole church!

As much as legalists and modern-day Pharisees hate to admit, the Holy Spirit is "ecumenical," filling anyone who will believe and ask. What does that mean? It means, if you are Catholic or Methodist or Episcopalian or Church of Christ or not even affiliated with a church, you can receive the Baptism right now!

Just out of Bible College, my first ministry was as a youth pastor in San Bruno, California. The pastor, Gerald Roles, was a Spirit-filled man who conducted a Spirit Life Clinic every Tuesday at 10:00 a.m. in the church basement. Mostly Catholics from the church down the street attended. They were so hungry for the filling of the Spirit, and to hear the Word of God, they came expecting great things, and the Lord never disappointed them. We never asked if they were saved; we just taught about the Baptism, laid on hands, and they received.

THERE ARE TWO BIBLICAL WAYS TO RECEIVE THE BAPTISM

1. You can be filled with the Holy Spirit on your own (Acts 2 and 10), or
2. Some may need instruction and the laying on of hands (Acts 8 and 19). For many, biblical instruction is necessary and wise. Otherwise, people might not have a clue what they have received.

In the old days of Pentecost we'd give an invitation, and a seeker would come to the altar and be flanked by the pastor on one side saying "Let go, brother. Just let go…let go…let go!" Someone on the other side, usually a deacon, was saying, "Hang on, brother. Just hang on…hang on…hang on!" People didn't know whether to let go or hang on and nothing ever happened.

Others thought they had to be "slain in the Spirit" to receive. Please understand, the Holy Spirit won't zap your power in order to give you power.

One young man was at the altar praying in tongues, and my friend went over and said, "You've got it." "I do?" "Yes!" "I've been praying like that for the past month. But I thought when I got it, I would be lifted 12 feet off the ground and spin around in the air."

Listen, when you get a weird idea of what it takes to receive the Baptism, you make God responsible to do something that is not Biblical, and then you are disappointed when it doesn't happen the way you think it should.

Chapter Three

DO YOU HAVE TO BE EMOTIONAL TO RECEIVE?

WELL, IF THAT WERE THE CASE, there would be a lot of unemotional believers who never receive.

Sometimes when people receive, they aren't sure it happened until one of us confirms that they've received, even though they are speaking in tongues. I've actually had to tell people that they had the Baptism in the Holy Spirit.

Someone asks, "So, how do you feel?" It doesn't matter how you feel, just obey the Word of God.

Remember, tongues are the evidence of the Baptism in the Holy Spirit, not joy, or any other feeling. Those will all come as you enjoy the fullness of the Spirit.

When hands are laid on you, you may experience *"stammering lips."*

> *"For with stammering lips and another tongue He will speak to this people, to whom He said, "This is the rest with which You may cause the weary to rest, and this is the refreshing;" yet they would not hear." (Isaiah 28:11)*

Do you know what stammering lips mean? It is an indication that another language is present inside you.

If, at that moment, you would not hinder it, and not keep speaking English (or your native language), but speak out anything else, you would be speaking in tongues that quickly. It's that simple.

Don't try to understand it. You don't. Don't decide how you are going to do it. You can't. Just do it.

> *"The spirits of the prophets are subject to the prophets." (I Corinthians 14:32)*

This is a key verse. You control when you speak, because you are in command of your own spirit at all times. You can decide to do it or you can decide not to do it. It is a matter of the will. God does not force you to speak.

When you take it like that by faith, you'll get all the joy you need and all the feelings, in time. But please understand, when you receive, you don't have all of God. It's just the beginning and a place to enter the fullness of the Spirit.

Read Acts 10—Cornelius, a Roman Centurion had character and integrity. God respects honest men. Cornelius prayed much and gave alms to the poor.

Here is a principle: If we do what God reveals to us, He will give us more. But if we don't obey the Lord, He is under no obligation to give us any more.

An angel appeared to Cornelius. It was a direct intervention. The angel gave him names and places and dates. Peter, on the other hand, was waiting for lunch, fell into a trance, and had a vision of some un-Kosher creepy crawlies which God said to "kill and eat." While he was contemplating and complaining about this vision, the Lord told him he had visitors, and to go with them. Peter went with Cornelius' servants, came to his house, realized that God did not show favoritism, started preaching the Gospel, and before he even got to the altar call, Cornelius and his whole household were filled with the Spirit and began to speak with tongues. (No formality, no ritual, not even laying on of hands…just simple faith.)

In Acts 11, Peter was called on the carpet for going to the Gentiles. (That's why he brought six Jewish believers with him.) In his defense, he said,

> *"And as I began to speak, the Holy Spirit fell upon them, as on us at the beginning. Then I remembered the word of the Lord, how He said, "John indeed baptized with water, but you shall be baptized with the Holy Spirit. If therefore God gave them the same*

gift as He gave us when we believed on the Lord Jesus Christ, who was I that I could withstand God?" (Acts 11:16, 17)

The gift of tongues was the evidence that they had received the Baptism.

Every Gospel account tells us that Jesus Christ will *"baptize you with the Holy Spirit"* (Mattew 3:11; Mark 1:8; Luke 3:16; John 1:33). It's very clear.

The Baptism with the Holy Spirit may be received immediately at the time of salvation (as with Cornelius' family—Acts 10), or at a later time. But nothing says you have to wait any amount of time to receive.

In a normally functioning church, every believer can and should receive the Baptism in the Holy Spirit. Why some want to be saved and have little or no power to follow and serve the Lord, I don't understand.

On the Day of Pentecost, Peter said,

"Repent, and let every one of you be baptized in the name of Jesus Christ

for the remission of sins; and you shall receive the gift of the Holy Spirit." (Acts 2:38)

Then Peter said:

"For the promise is to you and to your children, and to all who are afar off, as many as the Lord our God will call." (Acts 2:39)

That's you and me today.

But the Baptism in the Holy Spirit has been allowed to drop out of sight, even in Pentecostal churches. We need to claim our privilege back, not just today, or during a revival service, but people need to be assured that they can come to any Bible-believing church and receive the Baptism in the Holy Spirit, whenever and wherever.

The great irony is that many non-Pentecostal people are getting the Baptism ahead of us!

My older brother, Greg, moved out to California about 60 miles south of the small Assemblies of God church I was pastoring. Every Sunday, he'd drive up to church and have Sunday lunch with us. One Sunday after eating, he asked if he could become a member of our church (good cooking has a way of motivating some people). As much as I loved seeing him and watching him grow, I said "No," and that he needed to attend a local church near his home. So I gave him a pastor friend's name. But I asked Greg if he had received the Baptism since he'd been saved about two years earlier. He said he had not. We weren't brought up to know anything about the Baptism so he didn't have a clue what that was.

I went through the teaching while sitting on our couch, and asked if I may pray for him to receive. He said "Yes." We knelt at the couch, I laid hands on him, and without hesitation, he began speaking in tongues. (He did not have to unlearn all the weird ideas many church people have come to believe.) Suddenly, the tears began to flow; tears of joy and tears of cleansing. The Lord was washing his heart out and he confessed that he had always been jealous of me, in school, art and music. Then my tears started to flow and I confessed that I had always been jealous of him, in sports and sports and sports. Today, he is preaching the Gospel at his church and being a powerful witness in his community.

Now, when hands are laid on people, they receive the Baptism in the Spirit and the gift of tongues. It's simple, and the most *natural supernatural* thing that can happen to you.

When hands are laid on you, and you sense "stammering lips," just go with it, focus on praising the Lord for His goodness, don't hinder it, and you will be speaking in tongues that quickly.

Stammering lips is the Holy Spirit prompting you to speak out in tongues. He will not speak for you or through you but will prompt you to speak out. I've found that if you speak out loudly the tongues come easier. But God will not do it for you. He will not violate your free will or your personality.

Sadly, some people don't receive when hands are laid on them because they insist on speaking in English. "Glory, glory, glory, glory." "I love you, Jesus. I love you, Jesus." That's as much "in the flesh" as anything else.

> *"For if I pray in a tongue, my spirit prays, but my understanding is unfruitful. What is the conclusion then? I will pray with the spirit, and I will also pray with the understanding. I will sing with the spirit, and I will also sing with the understanding." (I Corinthians 14:14, 15)*

Paul made a clear distinction between praying and singing with our understanding, and praying and singing in the Spirit. Don't fight the Holy Spirit, because He will never go against your will.

Our Western culture demands to be in control of everything. But if you're afraid of letting the Holy Spirit prompt you to speak out and fill you to overflowing, you will never receive your gift.

Your mind or flesh will tell you "you're making it up yourself." Well, it is you because I Corinthians 14:32 says—"*The spirits of the prophets are subject to the prophets.*"

There is no mystery or secret here. It is you who is speaking, and the more you obey the prompting of the Holy Spirit, the more your language in the Spirit will flow.

Let me illustrate this by saying, suppose I am speaking at your church and you are sitting on the front row. I point you out and say, "Would you please stand for a minute" while signaling with my two fingers to stand. Most people would oblige because I prompted them to stand. I didn't lift you with my two fingers, did I? I merely signaled you. That's what the Holy Spirit does when we are baptized in the Spirit and filled to overflowing. He signals or prompts us to speak out in praise. For some, it is as easy as breathing. For others, it is so new, they resist and don't receive.

Please understand, you do not lose control of yourself, regardless of the old-time Pentecostal antics of emotionalism. You can decide to do it or decide not to do it. But stepping out in faith is always a requirement to receive anything from God.

> *"But without faith it is impossible to please Him, for he who comes to God must believe that He is, and that He is a rewarder of those who diligently seek Him." (Hebrews 11:6)*

I believe there are some people reading this right now, who can put this book down, let faith rise up in your heart, start praising the Lord Jesus Christ, be filled with the Spirit and start speaking in tongues in a matter of seconds.

Some may object: "But I don't have enough faith." If you are surrounded by

praying believers, you can use their faith.
That's scriptural. We pray for healing and
ask others to believe for us, don't we?

> *"Is anyone among you sick? Let him
> call for the elders of the church, and let
> them pray over him, anointing him
> with oil in the name of the Lord. And
> the prayer of faith will save the sick...."*
> (James 5:14, 15)

Even through the pages of this book,
you can borrow my faith, step out, start
praising Jesus Christ and begin to speak in
other tongues. I am agreeing with you in
prayer.

Chapter Four

DOES THE HOLY SPIRIT SPEAK THROUGH YOU?

I S GOD A VENTRILOQUIST? HE DOES not speak in tongues—you do. Paul wrote:

"If I pray in a tongue, my spirit prays"
(1 Corinthians 14:14)

Not the Holy Spirit. "My spirit." This misconception has caused many seekers to walk away empty, because they thought God would move their lips, mouth and vocal chords.

You are responsible for speaking in tongues, not God. If you knew how much the Lord wants to fill you right now, you might just start speaking out in your new language right where you sit.

If it was all the Holy Spirit, we would never have any mistakes, would we? And if we never made any mistakes, we'd never have I Corinthians 14, would we? That whole chapter was correcting the abuse of tongues in the church. (You can only be assured of never making any mistakes if you never do anything, and that would be a mistake in itself).

> *"They began to speak in tongues, as the Holy Spirit prompted them."* (Acts 2:4)

Now, from experience, we've learned that people cannot speak with their mouths closed. Some will come at the invitation to be baptized in the Spirit, scrunch up their face, and purse their lips waiting for God to make them say something. It doesn't work that way. Faith is a risk. Take the risk, and speak out. The Holy Spirit will prompt you (perhaps with stammering lips, or just a word or two), and you must take the next step, which is to speak out by faith.

Chapter Five

MYTHS AND
MISCONCEPTIONS

L ET ME TAKE A MINUTE TO DISPEL
some misconceptions about the Baptism:

MYTH 1: "You have to speak a lot of words
to get it." Why? How many words?
When I initially received, I spoke only
3 or 4 words, but I knew something
wonderful had happened. As I prac-
ticed my gift, it became a fluent language that I speak every day. You may
start speaking one word. That's great!
Keep speaking, and it will begin to
flow.

MYTH 2: "It must be a clear speech."
What is a clear speech? Have you

heard some Chinese dialects, with their guttural sounds, or African dialects with their clicking? We don't know what "clear speech" is. But it's good to have someone with you who can confirm that you have received the Baptism, so you won't doubt your gift.

MYTH 3: "If you have to copy someone else, that's in the flesh." Sometimes I don't feel like praying. I know I should. So, I start out in the flesh. If I keep at it, I get "in the spirit." I do the same with praising God. I prime the pump, and the joy follows.

"But you are not in the flesh but in the Spirit, if indeed the Spirit of God dwells in you…." (Romans 8:9)

In fact, those who suggest someone is "in the flesh" when they are seeking the Baptism are in the flesh for being so negative.

Myth 4: "I'm afraid it might be me." Of course it will be you. The Holy Spirit doesn't speak in tongues; He merely prompts you to. Those who think they are making it up don't understand the Scriptures, or the operation of the Spirit. Paul said,

"If I pray in an unknown tongue, MY spirit prays." (I Corinthians 14)

MYTH 5: "If it's of the Lord, it has to be perfect." That sounds noble and all, but God is dealing with flawed vessels who make plenty of mistakes. You may not have received before, but this time you will. And the more you use your prayer language, the more the Lord will perfect it and edify you.

MYTH 6: "You have to be careful of too much emotionalism." It's difficult to be touched by God and not get excited! But what do you mean, "Be careful?" How careful do you have to be to receive anything from the Lord? I say, let's be careful not to grieve or quench the Holy Spirit.

MYTH 7: "You shouldn't have to be coached into it." Well, did someone lead you in the "Sinner's Prayer" when you accepted Jesus? In the same way, you may be coached into the Baptism in the Holy Spirit and speaking in tongues. But what you do from that point on is between you and the Lord. How you begin is not as important as what you do with your gift every day. Let's get started, one way or another.

Chapter Six

MUST IT BE A REAL LANGUAGE?

I SUPPOSE SOMEONE CAN BE DECEITFUL and make up a babbling language. But that's not what we are talking about. We are talking about those who are seeking the Baptism by faith.

Who is to say whether or not a language is real? There are 6,000+ known dialects in the world today. More than 3,000 have been translated and 3,000 have not. Unless you know all 6,000 dialects then you can't call anything gibberish. You don't know.

Paul says there are *"tongues of men and of angels."* I Corinthians 14 states: *There is no sound without a meaning"* to God.

If someone is praying with you and you are reluctant to speak out, borrow a word from them. Prime the pump. It's not as important how one starts speaking, but that he just starts speaking out in faith.

Chapter Seven

CAN ONE RECEIVE A COUNTERFEIT GIFT?

SOME HAVE BEEN AFRAID TO SEEK THE Baptism and said, "But I might get the wrong experience—something from the Devil." Hey, what kind of God do we serve, anyway?

"If you being evil know how to give good gifts to your children, how much more will your heavenly Father give the Holy Spirit to those who ask Him?" (Luke 11:13)

Do not be afraid of what God has promised you. He will make sure there is an open heaven for you to believe and receive. And if you surround yourself with Bible-centered men and women of faith who have already received, you are in great company.

Chapter Eight

DOES THE DEVIL
SPEAK IN TONGUES?

THERE ARE NO FALSE TONGUES, AND the devil does not speak in tongues.

"A house divided against itself cannot stand." (Matthew 12:25)

There is nowhere in the Bible which speaks of a false tongue. If you are seeking the Holy Spirit, you will get the fullness of the Holy Spirit. There is no safer place for you to be than with God's people seeking the gift of the Holy Spirit

The Devil is putting fear in the hearts of believers—fear of receiving God's gifts, God's promises, the Baptism and tongues. You may have received years ago, and haven't done a thing with it since—because of fear. Paul warned Timothy:

> *"For God has not given us the spirit of fear, but of power, of love and of a sound mind." (2 Timothy 1:7)*

> *"The thief comes to steal, kill and destroy, but I have come that they may have life, and life more abundantly." (John 10:10)*

In the Bible, there are false miracles and false prophets, but never false tongues. Listen, if you talk in tongues, rejoice. You've got it! Enjoy God. Once you speak in tongues, you can do it the rest of your life. It's a gift,

> *"and the gifts and calling of God are without repentance." (Romans 11:29)*

To clear up any confusion, Christians cannot be demon-possessed. We can fall into sin, and be demon-harassed, but our body is the TEMPLE OF THE HOLY SPIRIT (I Corinthians 6:19). And you can be sure a demon isn't going to hang around the Holy Spirit!

There is a whole life of living in the Spirit, hearing His whisper, and walking in a new anointing of faith and power. But you have to receive the Baptism before you can have that life. This is where it starts.

Chapter Nine

IS HOLINESS NECESSARY FOR THE BAPTISM?

WELL, THAT POSES ANOTHER QUEStion: If so, how holy do you have to be? Some think that a certain degree of holiness is necessary to receive the Baptism. Have you ever heard someone say, "The Lord won't fill an unclean vessel?" Ask them where it says that in Scripture.

If God isn't going to fill an unclean vessel, we ought to close the doors of our churches and go golfing or fishing on Sundays.

What is holiness? And how holy do you need to be? The Bible says,

"our righteousness is as filthy rags." (Isaiah 64:6)

Holiness is not perfection. You can't be good enough to be baptized in the Holy Spirit.

"If we say that we have no sin, we deceive ourselves, and the truth is not in us." (1 John 1:8)

Being baptized in the Holy Spirit is NOT a sign that you are perfect. It just means that God loves you and gave you the gift of His Spirit.

For too long, we have held up the Baptism as a goal we must attain. "I FINALLY GOT IT!" They thought that was the end. And, for them, it was.

Some folks from the old holiness backgrounds believe that you can get to a stage where you never sin anymore. Well, if that was true, you'd have it made in the shade. But it doesn't work that way. Paul said,

"the flesh lusts against the Spirit, and the Spirit against the flesh." (Galatians 5:17)

You will always have that battle as long as you are with us.

So, you can't be good enough to receive the Baptism. The same way you received salvation in Christ by grace through faith, you receive the Baptism in the Holy Spirit.

Whenever you see the word "holy" in the Bible, it either refers to God, or that which is set apart for God.

> *"But you are a chosen generation, a royal priesthood, a holy nation, His own special people, that you may proclaim the praises of Him who called you out of darkness into His marvelous light." (I Peter 2:9)*

You are holy because you have been chosen, not because you are perfect.

> *"Not by works of righteousness which we have done, but according to His mercy He saved us, through the washing of regeneration and renewing of the Holy Spirit, whom He poured out on us abundantly through Jesus Christ our Savior." (Titus 3:5, 6)*

Let's say I have two hymnals sitting on the piano. One, we are going to use in the worship service. It is holy. But looking at it, some kid has scribbled on most of the pages, and other pages have been torn out. It is not perfect, but it is holy, because we chose it. Now, the other book is brand new, still in the wrapper. It is perfect, but not holy, because it is not chosen. The first book is like most of us. Our pages have been scribbled all over, and we may be missing some things upstairs, but God calls us HOLY because HE has chosen us. Now, when you get that in your spirit, you are going to feel like a million dollars, tax-free. PRAISE GOD!

> *"I say then: Walk in the Spirit, and you shall not fulfill the lust of the flesh. For the flesh lusts against the Spirit, and the Spirit against the flesh; and these are contrary to one another, so that you do not do the things that you wish. But if you are led by the Spirit, you are not under the law....But the fruit of the Spirit is love, joy, peace, longsuffering,*

kindness, goodness, faithfulness, gentleness, self-control. Against such there is no law. And those who are Christ's have crucified the flesh with its passions and desires. If we live in the Spirit, let us also walk in the Spirit." (Galatians 5:16-25)

Chapter Ten

HOW OLD MUST ONE BE?

I USED TO THINK THAT YOUNGER CHIL-
dren would not know how to receive or
understand the purpose of the Baptism.
But recently, at one of our Spirit Life
Clinics, during the invitation, a mother
brought down her 12-year-old daughter
and two boys, 8 and 6 years old. The sister
received beautifully, but the boys just
stood there looking at me as I prayed for
them. Clint Pruett, who has helped me in
a number of clinics, crouched down and
assured the boys that it was alright and
they would receive when they were ready.
The next Sunday, we were back and gave
another invitation at which the brothers
came forward, were prayed for, and they

readily received the fullness of the Spirit. I can only imagine the conversation around the dinner table the whole week before, when the sister talked about her new gift!

> *"Out of the mouth of babes and nursing infants, You have perfected praise." (Mattew 21:16)*

It is not for me to limit the power and gifts of God when someone, including a child, seeks them with all his heart.

Chapter Eleven

WHY SPEAK IN TONGUES?

MOST OF US FEEL UNCOMFORTABLE when others speak in a language we don't understand. The idea of speaking in tongues has caused more problems in today's church because many believers don't know why God gave us this gift. It is easier to just ignore it, or say that it is no longer a part of today's church, than to learn about it, teach believers its proper use, and watch them grow in all the gifts.

One reason for tongues can be found in James 3:6-8,

> "And the tongue is a fire, a world of iniquity. The tongue is so set among our members that it defiles the whole body, and sets on fire the course of

nature; and it is set on fire by hell. For every kind of beast and bird, of reptile and creature of the sea, is tamed and has been tamed by mankind. But no man can tame the tongue. It is an unruly evil, full of deadly poison."

No man can tame the tongue, but God can! Speaking in tongues is our way of surrendering that little member of our body, letting our minds take a back seat, and allowing the fullness of the Spirit to flow through us in prayer, praise and joy.

Another reason for tongues is found in I Corinthians 12 and 14. In 14:2 Paul writes: *"For he who speaks in a tongue does not speak to men but to God"*—prayer and praise. Praying in tongues is more direct and more in line with God's will.

"Likewise the Spirit also helps in our weaknesses. For we do not know what we should pray for as we ought, but the Spirit Himself makes intercession for us with groanings which cannot be uttered. Now He [God the Father]

*who searches the hearts knows what
the mind of the Spirit is, because He
makes intercession for the saints
according to the will of God."
(Romans 8:26,27)*

This is one way to pray AND NEVER
MISS GOD'S WILL.

Now, a point that is used in Debating
is a "consistency of terms." We all have to
agree on what certain terms mean. *"Praying in the spirit"* (I Corinthians 14:15)
will mean the same thing every time you
see it in the New Testament. It will mean
"praying in tongues."

Some might argue, "Praying in the
spirit" means ardent or fervent prayer.
That's not correct.

*"But you, beloved, building yourselves
up on your most holy faith, praying in
the Holy Spirit." (Jude 20)*

Almost all of my illustrations in this
book are my own experiences or come
from close and reliable sources. But this
story I heard in passing, which shows the

power of speaking in tongues, even when one has strayed from the Lord:

A west-coast evangelist had backslidden, and went back to drinking. He would sit at the end of bar, have a few drinks and start speaking in tongues. But after a few weeks of doing this, the Lord actually used those tongues to shake him up. He finally confessed his sin, came back to the Lord, and is still serving God.

You see, praying in the spirit can do something for you, even in a bar! God didn't cast him aside, but we would have. I'm glad our Father is more merciful than we are, aren't you?

> *"praying always with all prayer and supplication in the Spirit…"*
> *(Ephesians 6:18)*

That's part of the Armor of God.
Our praying is very limited, isn't it? Really. Most of our prayers are fairly selfish. But when you "pray in the Spirit," there is no end to what you can accomplish in the Lord.

Actually, "praying in the Spirit" is a COMMAND. And a command by God will only be given if there is the possibility of carrying it out. (You may want to do a Bible study on all the New Testament Commands given to believers, and realize that the Father will give you opportunities and the grace to meet each command).

> *"He who speaks in a tongue edifies himself..." "Edify" in Greek means "the constructive building up of the personality." (I Corinthians 14:4)*

In a recent letter, Dr. Carl R. Peterson, M.D., a Christian psychiatrist answered an inquiry about the health benefits of speaking in tongues:

EFFECTS OF EXTENDED VERBAL PRAYER AND JOYFUL LAUGHTER

"I have had a number of inquiries concerning the efficacy of praying in the spirit (glossolalia) and its benefit to the human immune system, i.e., immunity enhanced by chemicals released from a part of the brain. I am attempting to clarify some information I have shared with a number of ministers. This is information that may be deduced from what we know about the way the brain functions. We do know the part of the brain affected most noticeably by extended prayer and laughter represents a significant portion of the brain and its metabolic activity. Therefore, voluntary speech during extended vocal prayer causes a major stimulation in these parts of the brain (mainly the hypothalamus). The hypothalamus has direct regulation of four major systems of the body, mainly:

- » The pituitary gland and all target endocrine glands;
- » The total immune system;
- » The entire autonomic system; and
- » The production of brain hormone called endorphins and enkephalons, which are chemicals the body produces and are 100-200 times more powerful than morphine.

In summary, a very significant percentage of the central nervous system is directly and indirectly activated in the process of extended verbal and musical prayer over a period of time. This results in a significant release of brain hormones which, in turn, increases the body's general immunity. It is further enhanced through joyful laughter with increased respirations and oxygen intake to the brain, diaphragm and other muscles. This same phenomenon is seen in physical activity in general, i.e., running, etc.

We know from the Word of God that there is a true joy that builds and sustains.

Nehemiah tells us the joy of the Lord is our strength. There is joy in the presence of Jehovah. We, as believers having entered into that wonderful presence of our Lord, know this to be true. What we must continue to remember is that the joy of the Lord spoken of in the Word is so much more than any manifestation. We can truly have that unspeakable joy in the face of any trials we may encounter, if our joy is grounded in a knowledge of the Lord Jesus Christ.

I hope the above information helps to clarify the report you received regarding my statement in the area of the physical effects of speaking in tongues and joyful laughter for extended periods of time. Truly, we all benefit—body, soul, and spirit—from obedience and yielding to the Spirit of God in every area of our lives."

This is why the disciples came out of the upper room speaking in tongues and were accused of being drunk (Acts 2:13). They were speaking and laughing!

Speaking in tongues is evidence of the Spirit of God working in our unconscious, and bringing together body, soul and spirit as God inhabits our praises. In other words—praying in tongues is GOOD FOR OUR HEALTH.

When we come to the Lord, we don't always know what our real need is. But praying in tongues perfects our prayer *"according to the will of God."*

That's why Paul said,

"I thank God I speak with tongues more than you all." (I Corinthians 14:18)

"I wish you all spoke with tongues..." (I Corinthians 14:5)

How could Paul desire this? Only if it is a gift that is granted to ALL God's people. It is for everybody or it is for nobody, for God does not show favoritism.

Here's a little secret: Tongues speaking is a way to praise God without inhibition. Your mind isn't getting in the way. You are worshiping the Lord under an open heaven.

A lot of people, when they receive the gift, because they cannot measure its effectiveness at the time, fail to realize how important it is. But if you come back one year from now after using your gift daily in prayer and praise, then tell me where you are with the Lord.

Let me give you an example: Have you ever doubted your salvation? If you are a thinking person, you have. We all have at one point or another. The same thing will happen with speaking in tongues. The devil will try to rob you of your blessing. Don't let him. Keep it up. Pray in the spirit and sing in the spirit!

When you are baptized in the Holy Spirit you can look back and say, "I know this happened to me, for I heard myself speaking in tongues."

Now, I've been a student at a non-Pentecostal seminary. Don't you think I've heard all the reasons why I should never speak in tongues? Did I quit? No one could ever show me in Scripture that I should not speak in tongues. Instead, I showed them that they should, and some even did.

When I was pastoring a small church in the Napa Valley, there was a family that were members of our church. But only the wife, son and daughter attended.

The father was a retired U.S. Navy Captain. The son-in-law was a student at a local seminary studying for the ministry. I invited my former chaplain, Dr. Stanford E. Linzey, to come and do a revival.

We had about 80 people in our whole church. It was a long trip from Southern California, but Linzey believed that when "one of my boys calls," he would come running. He came, and discovered that this was foreordained of the Lord, because the retired Captain was his former Commanding Officer from NAS Moffett Field, just south of San Francisco. Harry Sorensen heard that Chaplain Linzey was in town, so he came to the meetings, and so did his fundamentalist son-in-law.

When Chaplain Linzey finished the revival in our little church three days later, twenty two people had been baptized in the Holy Spirit, including his former CO, Captain Harry Sorensen and his son-in-law, Gary. Gary later told me, "I'm not going back to the seminary. I'm going to find a school that teaches the Full Gospel."

Chapter Twelve

IS THERE ANY POWER IN PRAYING IN TONGUES?

I WILL ANSWER THAT QUESTION WITH A short story. For many years, Rev. Paul Schoch was the pastor of an Assemblies of God church in downtown Oakland, California. One day he was called to the bedside of a dying middle-aged woman. He came and knelt down at her bed. He prayed a typical pastor's prayer at a time like this but didn't feel finished, so he started praying in tongues. After about five minutes, he was jolted from his prayer by the woman sitting up in her bed, very healthy, and shouting at him, "Why did you do it? Why did you do it!?" With eyes wide opened, he asked, "Do what?!"

She then told him that while he was praying she died and started going upward. She saw a bright light and the closer she got to it she realized it was Jesus. But while she was still some distance from Him she heard Pastor Schoch's prayer coming to the Throne of Grace in English saying, "Dear Lord, our sister is not done here. Please spare her life. Give her more time with us."

And suddenly, Jesus put up his hand, and the woman said, "I turned around and started coming back and I could see through the roof, and there you were praying at my bedside in tongues! Why did you do it?!"

You have no idea what you can accomplish in the will of God when you pray in tongues, because—

"He [the Holy Spirit] makes intercession for the saints according to the will of God." (Romans 8:27)

Chapter Thirteen

WHAT COMES AFTER
THE BAPTISM?

🪽

THAT IS A LEGITIMATE QUESTION SINCE so many people stop at the initial gift of tongues and don't know what to expect from the Lord. But all the gifts you read about in I Corinthians 12 and 14 are available to every believer.

The Baptism is just the beginning. It is NOT salvation but a gift for those who are saved to give them power for service.

When one is born again, God gives him a new nature,

> *"Old things are passed away. All things have become new." (2 Corinthians. 5:17)*

The Baptism opens up a new dimension for every believer. When you are baptized in the Holy Spirit, you have the same experience the Apostles had in the first century church.

Acts 1:8, "you shall receive power...." In the Greek, it means every time the Holy Spirit comes upon you, you shall receive power, not just once, or once and for all.

> *"And do not be drunk with wine...but be filled with the Spirit, speaking to one another in psalms and hymns and spiritual songs, singing and making melody in your heart to the Lord, giving thanks always for all things to God the Father in the name of our Lord Jesus Christ, submitting to one another in the fear of God." (Ephesians 5:18-21)*

That means a daily "filling" with the Spirit. And then Paul tells us how, by singing songs of praise to God and giving thanks.

Jesus said,

"He who believes in Me, the works that I do he will do also; and greater works than these he will do, because I go to My Father." (John 14:12)

When Jesus went to His Father He sent us the indwelling Holy Spirit who can and will do the same and greater works in us and through us. Yes, that can mean praying for the sick and having them healed in Jesus' Name, including miracles, words of knowledge and wisdom, even raising the dead! When we are led by the Spirit there is no limit to how the Lord can use us.

Living in the realm of the Spirit means living under the "Crucifixion Principle"—

"I have been crucified with Christ; it is no longer I who live, but Christ who lives in me; and the life which I now live in the flesh, I live by the faith of the Son of God, who loved me and gave Himself for me." (Galatians 2:20)

When this principle governs our daily lives, even our outlook is eternity-based. In Ecclesiastes 3:11 Solomon wrote: *"He has put eternity in their hearts…"*

When one is filled with the Spirit he wants to lead others to Christ. That's just how the Lord works in us. The Church needs to encourage those who receive to pray for opportunities to share their faith as the Spirit leads them.

How do we know when we are being led by the Spirit? If we know we are right with God and living in the Spirit, God will often give us "hunches," "nudges," or a "tug in our hearts" to do something. If that tug persists after praying about it, you know that it is the Holy Spirit and should step out in faith.

Chapter Fourteen

KNOWING THE WILL OF GOD

I HAVE LEARNED THERE ARE AT LEAST five biblical ways to know the will of God (short of an angelic visitation or hearing the voice of God). This is not a legalistic formula, but these are arrows to lead one along the path with Jesus:

1. Does the Bible back it up? (Is it Scriptural?)
2. Do you have the inner witness of the Holy Spirit when you pray about it?
3. Does the Church confirm it to be God's leading? (They are our checks and balances).
4. Are circumstances giving you an open or closed door?

5. Does your spouse agree with you for it? (Never underestimate the wisdom of a praying spouse).

Sometimes being led by the Spirit simply means you do what needs to be done, and as you do, the Lord shows you more steps to take.

I served my country for more than three years on an aircraft carrier. It weighed 68,000 tons. The rudder weighed 90,000 pounds. But that huge rudder did no good when the ship was tied to the pier. Only when it was underway did that rudder steer the ship. Many of us need to be about our Father's business before the Lord will give us further leading.

In 2003, Carolyn and I had been praying for her to get back into education and be a principal again, which was her gift. For two years she looked and looked for an open position. Nothing. At that time we wanted to move to a different house so we put our house on the market. A couple came to ask if we wanted to rent it out.

We said, "No," but we made friends with them and found out he was on the board of Legacy Christian Academy one mile down the street. Carolyn said she wanted to get back into education. He said, "Send me your resume." The school was just about to hire another principal, and at the last minute, they hired Carolyn. She became the Lower School Principal and then the Dean for eight years. How many jobs have come to your front door like that?

I can't speak for anyone else, so let me share some ways the Lord has shown Himself powerful through spiritual gifts in our lives.

BOLDNESS IN THE SPIRIT

After pastoring the small country church in the Napa Valley, California for three years, I think the people were getting tired of me and a "vote of confidence" had me at a 67% positive rating. (I was young and had a lot to learn about people and leadership). That next Sunday we were scheduled to have a church-wide potluck after the evening service. For the previous five weeks I had been preaching a series on the "Power of Praise."

Just before I walked up to the pulpit a trio of tough-looking bikers strolled into the church and sat right in the middle pew. About five minutes into my sermon on love the biker leader interrupted me and said, "Do you believe that, Preacher?" I said, "I sure do," and continued with my message. Another five minutes passed and he interrupted me again. I said, "Sir, the Lord has given me the message for this evening. If you would like to say something, when I'm finished you will have a chance." Another five minutes and he stood up and interrupted again! Immediately, the Holy Spirit spoke to my heart, "You are not dealing with flesh and blood. This is a battle in the spirit." And suddenly I was filled with a holy boldness

I had never known before. (I'm usually a lover not a fighter).

I stepped out of the pulpit, walked down the aisle within twelve feet of this biker, pointed my finger in his face and said, "I rebuke you in the Name of Jesus Christ and command you to leave this church now!" The man looked at me in shock. (Apparently he was not used to being spoken to that way). I walked back to the pulpit and he stepped into the aisle but just stood there. I said, "Ushers, this man is leaving right now!" Every man in the church stood up except one. (I didn't know I had so many "ushers," but men love a good fight). One man came over to this biker and grabbed his arm. I said, "No, don't touch him. He is leaving right now." The man's two cronies had already left, but he got to the back door, turned on his heels and started spouting profanities. Just then, without any prompting from me, the whole church broke out into loud praise where no one could hear this guy. Finally, I heard him shout over the praising crowd, "I'll be back!"

When our praise died down and the people took their seats, I said, "For the past five weeks I've been preaching on the power of praise and the Lord wanted to see if you learned anything." I leaned into the microphone and said, "You passed the test," and the church went wild.

Well, that potluck was one we will never forget because the people came to-gether to rally around me and give praise to God for protecting our church family. (I think my approval rating even went up a couple points, too).

HEALINGS

While pastoring that same church, I was asked to drive 25 miles to pray for a member's mother who was dying of ter-minal leukemia in the hospital. I drove to the Queen of the Valley Hospital in Na-pa, CA. I talked briefly with the mother, laid hands on her and prayed. I'm sorry to say that my prayer was more one of comfort in one's last hours of life than for a mighty healing. But God had other plans. Within two weeks, Jesus healed Pauline Smith completely of leukemia. The doctors had no explanation and called her their "miracle lady." During her hospital stay, her three grown daughters sold mom's home and divided up the furniture. When Pauline was released she had no place to live. Instead, she found a retirement inn that required each guest to be in good health with a letter from her doctor. She passed with flying colors!

Another one of our members was Gladys Hardcastle who was an elderly shut-in. I would visit her once a month. She had Parkinson's disease and said the only thing that would help her with the shaking was orange juice. Her refrigerator was filled with it. One day, when I was just about to leave, I said, "Gladys, let me pray for you." I grabbed both of her hands and prayed a simple pastor's prayer for comfort and peace. About four days later I received a phone call. The voice said, "I just had to check it out before I told you." I said, "Gladys, is that you?" She went on: "I am healed of Parkinson's disease!" I asked what happened. She said, "When you were here and took my hands to pray for me I felt electricity go right through my body. I knew I was healed instantly, but I wanted to get checked out by my doctor. When I went to my doctor of forty three years and asked him to run tests for Parkinson's, he reluctantly did so. After the tests he said, "Well, I don't know what happened to you Gladys, but you have no signs of Parkinson's!" She told him Jesus healed her. The doctor was not a believer and said, "Well, I don't know about that, but you're as fit as a fiddle. Now get out of my office. You're wasting my time!"

Gladys finished our phone conversation by saying, "I came right home and threw out all my orange juice!"

MIRACLE

Years ago, my family and I were driving back to California on Interstate 40, passing through Tucumcari, NM. That evening when we checked into a motel, it was 70 degrees out. When we woke up, there was 4" of snow on our car and it was coming down hard. By the time we got on the freeway, we were heading right into the blizzard and the road was a sheet of ice. Every time I tried to gain any speed, we slid onto the shoulder. About the third time, I said, "We need to pray." As we held hands I sensed a strong anointing from the Holy Spirit and my faith was so full. I remembered Jesus making the storm calm. I thought, "But that was Jesus." And the Lord said, "I am the same today and living inside you." With that I rebuked the storm in the Name of Jesus, commanding it to calm down. Do you know what happened? Nothing. Well, it seemed like nothing. The blizzard just got worse, but I crept back out onto the highway and started weaving my way through semis that were jackknifing, trucks that were running into campers, and hundreds of cars stuck on the shoulder. We drove 50 miles without any problem. That's when I realized the Lord had put a blizzard-proof bubble around us! We were one of the few that made it through without an accident.

SPIRIT OF DISCERNMENT

We had an opportunity to invest in the oil and gas industry here in Texas with a well-respected and successful friend and believer. But as we prayed about the Lord's leading we both got "red flags." I couldn't understand. Everything lined up for a good investment but we knew that we needed to obey the Spirit. Within two years that same man was convicted of fraud and sent to jail for 20 years!

PROPHECY

In our church in St. Helena, I would always give an altar call after the message.

One day a woman came forward and said she had an unspoken request. I laid hands on her and began to prophesy words that I could almost see in front of her, that out of her "belly shall come forth springs of living water, and the new life she had been praying for." Well, she began to cry uncontrollably, and I went on to pray for someone else. A few weeks passed and I got a call from her. She asked if I remembered praying for her, and I did. She said, "Pastor, what you didn't know is that I had been praying to get pregnant, but knew it would have to be a miracle since my husband had had a vasectomy from his previous marriage. When you prophesied over me, I knew God heard my prayer, and I'm calling to say that I'm pregnant!"

Conclusion

LET'S RECAP THE MAIN POINTS OF BE-
ing baptized in the Holy Spirit:

» Joel 2:28 / Acts 2:38,39 - "the promise is for everyone who calls on the Lord."

» No emotion is necessary (many fear losing control, or being too emotional)

» You are not better than those who haven't received, you are just better than you were before.

» The Holy Spirit does not speak through you—He merely prompts you to speak in tongues. You are always in control.

» Your tongue is not babbling, nor does it have to be a known language.

» You can never be "good enough" to receive the Baptism, but you are holy because you have been chosen in Christ.

» Once you've spoken in tongues, you can do it the rest of your life.

PURPOSE OF TONGUES: (P-E-P-SI)

» **P**ower to be a witness for Jesus Christ (Acts 1:8).
» **E**dify yourself in the faith (Jude 20). God inhabits our praises.
» **P**ray the perfect will of God (Romans 8:26).
» **S**piritual **I**nfillings will follow the Baptism *(I Corinthians 12:7-11—word of wisdom, word of knowledge, faith, gifts of healings, miracles, prophecy, discernment of spirits, different tongues, and interpretation of tongues).*

In the Last Days we are going to see a greater outpouring of the Holy Spirit and spiritual gifts in the Church. How important is the Church? God will not do anything substantial in you or through you APART from your relationship with His Bride.

Note: If you are using this as a guidebook to teach on the Baptism in the Holy Spirit, this would be a good time to ask the people to join you in prayer and singing praises to Jesus Christ, the King of kings, Lord of lords, and Author and Finisher of our faith. Then invite them to come up to receive the Baptism. Invite—

» The unsaved
» Those who received the Baptism years ago but haven't done anything since, and
» Those who want to be filled to overflowing for the first time with the initial evidence of speaking in other tongues.

Then believe God to honor your faith, back up His Word, meet His promises, change lives, and enjoy your Second Blessing, for *"you shall receive power after the Holy Spirit comes upon you!"*

TESTIMONIALS

"I would recommend to any pastors who are considering hosting Pastor Kurt Stratton's *Spirit Life Clinic* to do so. We at Community Life Church have been very pleased with the teaching and the fruit of Pastor Kurt's ministry. We hosted the clinic on a Saturday in late August and are already looking forward to hosting it again in six months. The teaching removes the misconceptions and poor theology that so many have been exposed to and replaces it with sound biblical doctrine. Our people responded to the invitation given by Kurt after his teaching and half of those in attendance received the baptism in the Holy Spirit with the evidence of speaking in tongues!

Since then, it has been a joy to see the fruit of the Spirit so evidenced in the lives and families of those who attended the clinic. For some, it was a refresher; for others, it was new and informative; but for all, it was well received and inspirational. We have seen men step up and into their roles and responsibilities of the households. We have seen genuine repentance and reconciliation between generations in families. Basically we are witnessing the promise of the scripture for those who would believe and receive all that the Lord has for them.

We are grateful for Pastor Kurt's ministry and are looking forward to exposing more and more of our people to his ministry in the future."

—Pastor Mike Banas, Senior Pastor, Community Life Church, McKinney, TX

"Connie and I loved the *Spirit Life Clinic* Kurt conducted. Truths of the Baptism in the Holy Spirit from the Bible were expressed in ways that were easily understood, and Kurt's passion for teaching was contagious. I re-learned things that I had forgotten and now I am again using my spiritual language."

—Clint Pruett, former Director of
Evangelism Explosion Intl.,
Southwest Region

"Kurt Stratton has a new, fresh and non-threatening way to present a never-changing message in an ever-changing world. His "Spirit Life Clinic" is a perfect way to teach new, and not so new, Christians about the gift of the Holy Spirit. Every time he has taught the Spirit Life Clinic, people are filled with the Spirit. It's amazing! Our people have loved it. I strongly recommend that you invite Kurt Stratton to your church today."

—Kendall Bridges, Lead Pastor,
Freedom Life Church, Carrollton, TX

SPIRIT LIFE CLINIC

THE SPIRIT LIFE CLINIC TEAM
Carolyn and Kurt Stratton and
Clint and Connie Pruett

Kurt conducting a Spirit Life Clinic during Bible Study in the chapel at Freedom Life Church where twelve received the baptism of the Holy Spirit.

A Spirit Life Clinic on Saturday morning at
Community Life Church. 61 people attended a
3-hour concentrated session, and all 24 who
responded to the invitation received the Baptism.

BIOGRAPHY

Kurt D. Stratton is a Vietnam Veteran (1971-1974), having served onboard the U.S.S. Coral Sea (CVA-43) as a Radioman Second Class Petty Officer and Pentecostal/Charismatic Layleader. He was also a Chaplain in the U.S. Navy Reserves (1984-1986).

Kurt is a graduate of Bethany University in Santa Cruz, California with a B.S. degree in Ministry (and was honored to be the Graduation Speaker of 1978). He also studied at Golden Gate Baptist Theological Seminary in Mill Valley, California for his Master of Divinity degree.

Kurt was senior pastor of:

» Calvary Christian Center in St. Helena, California
» Trinity Community Church, San Rafael, California

- » New Life Community Church (co-pastor with Dr. P.T. Mammen), San Francisco, CA
- » Stonebrook Church, Frisco, Texas (he and his wife started it two days before 9/11).

Kurt has been the author of KURT'S DAILY MUSE, an Internet Daily Devotional, since 1996.

He and his wife, Carolyn, (who is the Head of School at Canyon Creek Christian Academy in Richardson, TX), are members of Gateway Church in Frisco, TX, and have four adult children and seven grandchildren.

Contact Kurt Stratton for a *Spirit Life Clinic* at the following:

12709 Grand Valley Drive
Frisco, TX 75033
Kdmuse1@gmail.com
(972) 370-0302

www.ingramcontent.com/pod-product-compliance
Lightning Source LLC
Chambersburg PA
CBHW071055040426
42443CB00013B/3343